IT WAS FRIDAY, and the day before Christmas Eve. It was also forty-five days after the 2022 midterm election. At the Alameda County Superior Courthouse in Oakland, California, the Registrar of Voters staff had weeks ago certified the election results.

Yet at some point that day, the office received startling news. According to an outside analysis, they had made a serious mistake. Actually, they had made a series of mistakes, throwing off the final vote totals in a myriad of races. And in one fiercely contested school board election, the Registrar had certified the wrong winner.

All this happened because of a novel election process known as *ranked-choice voting,* or RCV (sometimes called *instant runoff voting* or, in Canada, *alternative voting*). Used statewide in Alaska and Maine, and in some local elections in states like California, Utah, and Vermont, RCV is backed by a powerful national lobbying effort. It is part of an agenda that makes elections more complex and

T0005159

chaotic, and consequently less transparent and trustworthy.

WHAT IS RANKED-CHOICE VOTING?

In a normal election, each voter gets one vote in each race for a particular office. Votes are counted once (unless there is a recount). The candidate receiving the most votes wins. This is sometimes called a "first-past-the-post" election, because it is run once and the candidate who comes in first, i.e., with the most votes, wins the race.

In an RCV election, voters can rank multiple candidates, and vote counting can go through many rounds of adjusting and recounting before declaring a winner. Because of this,

---

In an RCV election, vote counting can go through many rounds of adjusting and recounting.

---

the ballot design, tabulation process, and reporting of election results are all different. Understanding these differences is important to evaluating the risks of RCV.

Ranking Candidates, or Not

Rather than voting for a single candidate, voters in an RCV election can rank some number of the candidates according to their preference. This number varies. In Minneapolis, voters are allowed to rank up to three candidates. In Alaska and New York City, voters can rank five. In Maine, voters can rank as many candidates as are on the ballot, plus a write-in candidate.

This leads to two different RCV ballot designs. Where ranking is limited to three, ballots typically present the list of candidates three times, in three columns. The first column is for the first preference vote, and so on. It appears as if there are three separate elections, all with the same candidates.

Where voters can rank more than three candidates, the names are usually listed just once down the left column. To the right of each name is a series of bubbles that can be filled in. The first bubble represents a first-preference vote, the second bubble a second-choice vote, and so on, moving from left to right. It was voter confusion with this kind of ballot, together with a tabulation error, that led to the RCV election failure in California.

Counting, and Counting, and Counting...

Tabulating RCV ballots is unlike any normal election process – unless one candidate receives a majority of first-preference votes. In that case, RCV is irrelevant and that candidate wins. Otherwise, a process of adjusting and retabulating the votes begins and is repeated as many times as is necessary to arrive at a winner under RCV rules.

When no candidate has a majority of first-preference votes, then the candidate with the fewest first-preference votes is eliminated. Or, in some RCV systems, all candidates without a mathematical possibility of winning are eliminated after the first tabulation. Ballots where an eliminated candidate was ranked first are now either adjusted or discarded. If there is a next-ranked candidate, that candidate is "moved up" and treated as the first-ranked candidate on that ballot for the next round of tabulation. If the voter did not rank another candidate, the ballot is discarded (this is called "ballot exhaustion").

In an election with two candidates, RCV never matters because one candidate will always have a majority in the first count. Add a third candidate, and RCV may require a second round of adjusting and counting. Add more candidates, and more rounds may be required. In New York City, the Democratic Party primary for mayor in 2021 included thirteen candidates and went through eight rounds of tabulation. The election for mayor of Oakland, California, in 2022 had ten candidates and required nine rounds of tabulation.

Where Did RCV Come From?

The impulse that produced RCV was directed at creating proportional representation rather than simply changing how officials are elected. (A proportional system represents political interest groups, rather than districts, and usually results in a multiparty system and coalition government.) In the 1850s, an English barrister and former Member of Parliament named Thomas Hare proposed a multiple-winner election system with votes transferred among candidates based on mathematical calculations. About two decades later, that system was modified by an American architect and academic to make it work for single-winner elections. The American's name was W. R. Ware, and what was originally called "Ware's System" is now known as RCV.

Most nations rejected their proposals, but versions of Ware's and Hare's systems were adopted in some Australian elections and in Ireland upon its independence. Members of Australia's House of Representatives have been elected using RCV since 1918 (although most elections are won in the first round). In the early twentieth century, some American cities adopted them for council elections, often as part of larger populist or progressive reform packages. All of these cities repealed RCV, often within less than a decade.

Who Wants RCV and Why?

A network of think tanks and advocacy organizations, predominantly on the political left, promote RCV in the United States today. What little support there is on the right seems mostly to come from disaffected Republicans rather than conservatives. This makes sense – an obvious reason to demand a rules change is losing under existing rules. That, and the related fear of losing future elections, explains much of the push for RCV in Alaska and Maine.

RCV backers claim it will reduce partisanship, make campaigns less negative, give voters more choices, and even save money. No doubt many of them believe some or all of these claims – this book will explain why each is incorrect. Some of the interest on the left also seems intertwined with the belief that, if a system is really democratic, their candidates will win, and thus if their candidates don't win, the system must be broken and in need of "reform."

The FairVote Network

The leading proponent of RCV is FairVote, a Maryland-based think tank. Founded in 1992 as Citizens for Proportional Representation, the group appears to focus most of its efforts today advocating for RCV at the local and state levels. Supporters of FairVote are a who's who of far-left donors, including George Soros's Open Society Foundations, several other Soros-connected foundations, the Arnold Foundation, and the Tides Foundation.

The website of FairVote's lobbying affiliate, FairVote Action, identifies itself as "the driving force for RCV." It lobbies directly and through affiliates in state legislatures and supports state and local ballot measures. FairVote Action claims credit for a statewide

Tabulating RCV ballots is unlike any normal election process.

measure in Maine and for "wins in dozens of cities around the nation, from Utah to New York City." Its website lists forty-two state and six local allied organizations, all focused on RCV.

Unite America: An RCV Money Machine

Another group advocating for RCV is Unite America, which claims to be "a movement of Democrats, Republicans, and independents." Unite America engages in political campaigns and makes grants to other organizations. Despite its claims to bipartisanship, its leadership tilts overwhelmingly towards the left. For example, its board of directors has three former members of Congress – two Democrats and one Republican. The latter is former Rep. Carlos Curbelo, who was the *most liberal* Republican in Congress at the end of his time in office, according to ratings by the American Conservative Union.

The founder of Unite America, Charles Wheelan, is an academic who ran unsuccessfully for Congress as a Democrat and has contributed to numerous other Democratic Party organizations and candidates. One of Unite America's top funders, and also co-chair of its board, is Kathryn Murdoch. The daughter of right-leaning media mogul Rupert Murdoch has not followed in her father's political footsteps, instead giving almost exclusively to Democratic candidates and campaign committees, with a focus on liberal environmental causes.

In 2019, *The New York Times* reported that Murdoch and her husband had "already invested millions" in Unite America. The glowing profile quoted Murdoch's description of the couple as "anchor funders" in a plan to raise "nine figures," with the *Times* helpfully pointing out that "the lowest nine-figure number is $100 million." Since then, Unite

America has supported RCV advocacy in Alaska, Colorado, Georgia, Massachusetts, Minnesota, Nevada, New Hampshire, New Mexico, New York, Oregon, Tennessee, Texas, Utah, Vermont, Virginia, Washington, Wyoming, and likely other states as well.

Katherine Gehl

Another major funder of RCV campaigns is Katherine Gehl, who advocates a more comprehensive   and radical – change to elections called "final-five voting." In 2015, Gehl sold her family's food business to a private equity company. She was already active in politics, having worked for Chicago Mayor Richard Daley and having been appointed by President Barack Obama to the board of the Overseas Private Investment Corporation.

In 2018, Gehl co-founded a Wisconsin group called Democracy Found to push Final-Five Voting there. Two years later, she co-authored *The Politics Industry: How Political Innovation Can Break Partisan Gridlock and Save Our Democracy* and presented a popular Ted

Talk. Both portray her plan as the only way to solve "our broken political and democratic system." She has served on the board of Unite America and runs her own national nonprofit, the Institute for Political Innovation.

Gehl's final-five voting proposal incorporates RCV into a scheme that would also eliminate political parties from the nominating process. Instead, a preliminary election would include all candidates regardless of party. It would be open to all voters, with each casting a single vote (this step does not use RCV). The five candidates with the most votes then advance to a final election that would use RCV to determine the winner.

A version of this plan, with four (rather than five) candidates advancing to the final election, became law in Alaska in 2020. Voters in Nevada passed a state constitutional amendment for final-five voting in 2022, with supporters outspending opponents more than ten to one. Gehl, the top donor, gave more than $6 million. Kathryn Murdoch gave $2.5 million. Because Nevada requires state constitutional amendments to pass in two successive general elections, it will only take effect if passed again in 2024.

THE RCV ATTACK ON POLITICAL PARTIES

RCV is often just a piece of a larger agenda to reduce or eliminate the role of political parties in elections. Reformers like Gehl have particular disdain for the two-party system, which she says has "plagued and perverted" our politics. The inventors of RCV and related voting systems wanted to create proportional representation – something FairVote continues to push today. It is important to recognize these proposals for what they are: serious challenges to the American political system.

In one sense, every democratic political system in the world is a two-party system: there is the coalition of those in power, and everybody else. No matter how many parties exist in a multi-party parliamentary system, only one gets the most votes, forms a government, and sees its leader become prime minister. If it brings other parties into a coalition, this means that after the election a small group of elites has cobbled together something comparable to an American political party.

Supporters of FairVote are a who's who of far-left donors.

In the United States, our major political parties *are* coalitions. The Democratic and Republican parties are continuously being cobbled together from the ground up: first in precincts; then in counties, legislative districts, and congressional districts; then in states. This coalition building is far more open and democratic than the alternative.

A stable party system also provides a check on demagogues. Party nominating contests add layers of scrutiny to the electoral process. This makes it much more difficult for a billionaire to convert his fortune into political power. Just ask Michael Bloomberg.

Unfortunately, the power of political parties has been under attack for decades. Campaign finance regulations have shifted spending from parties to non-partisan groups, like "super PACs," that are far less accountable for what they say and do. Primary elections have weakened the most basic power of parties to choose their own nominees, reducing their ability to vet potential public officials. RCV advocates decry the results of these past reforms but want to double down on the same mistakes.

Forcing RCV into Party Primaries

Another way these reformers attack political parties is by trying to force them to use RCV for primary elections. Their key talking point, at least to conservatives, is that the Virginia Republican Party used the system in 2021 to nominate their statewide candidates and then swept all three elections. It's a just-so story: Republicans were losing in Virginia until they used RCV, and suddenly you have Gov. Glenn Youngkin!

The story is silly for three reasons. First, the Virginia Republican Party only used RCV because of the COVID shutdowns. It was an emergency measure to replace its usual convention, which features multiple rounds of voting but also allows for deliberation and compromise during the process. Second, the convention-replacement use of RCV was not the equivalent of a primary election because it featured only 12,550 elected delegates.

The most important rebuttal, however, is the simple fact that Youngkin led in every round of ballot counting. In other words, RCV made no difference to the outcome. The same was true of the nominees for Lieutenant Governor and Attorney General.

If a political party chooses to use RCV to nominate candidates, as an emergency measure or otherwise, that should be within its power as a private organization. Forcing that decision on a political party oversteps the government's power. Neither should a political party that wants to use RCV force taxpayers and election administrators to bear that burden. After all, in Virginia, the Republicans ran the process on their own.

RCV Benefits Elites, Damages Democracy

The simple fact is that RCV makes it harder to vote. This is ironic, since much of its support comes from people who claim any voter identification requirement is so onerous that it violates basic civil rights. In fact, RCV might function like the literacy tests once used to keep immigrants and other undesirables away from the polls. Even supporters admit that massive public education campaigns are necessary to help voters navigate their strange new process.

The Oakland school board election debacle happened, in part, because of 235 confused voters. In that race, voters were offered four rankings: one for each of three candidates plus a write-in. To cast a valid vote, they could fill in between one and four of the twenty bubbles in the grid. Each of these voters, for reasons known only to themselves, failed to fill in a first-preference bubble. They did, however, rank a candidate second, and possibly also third and fourth.

In every election, voters make mistakes. Each mistake makes the election harder to administer. Some also leave voters disenfranchised. A sensible goal for election policy is to make it easy to vote and hard to make a mistake. RCV makes it harder to vote while creating new possibilities for voter errors.

RCV ballots are longer than normal ballots. Each race takes up more space, sometimes requiring an entire page for just one election. This means a ballot that might have

Final-five voting incorporates RCV into a scheme that would eliminate political parties from the nominating process.

fit on two sides of a page could require several additional sheets of paper. In each race, voters are asked to fill out more bubbles or boxes or lines. Candidates are listed in rows, preferences are listed in columns. It is all spread across the page, and includes more fine print and instructions than in a normal election.

Every additional bubble creates new opportunities for a stray mark, a missed vote, or a double vote (called an "overvote"). Any of these can result in a vote not counting or even an entire ballot being invalidated.

Consider another Alameda County election in 2022: the hotly contested race for mayor of Oakland. There were ten candidates (fewer than in the past), requiring nine rounds of counting. Election officials recorded 133,527 ballots. In the election for mayor, 5,081 of those ballots were left blank and 2,114 were discarded as overvotes. Another 810 were originally ignored because, as in the school board race, voters left blank the first-preference bubbles but did rank candidates in the race.

It is possible that voters intended not to vote in the race and thus chose to leave it blank. Whether because they were overwhelmed by a matrix of fifty bubbles or they disliked all ten candidates is impossible to know. For the 2,924 voters who either filled in two first-preference bubbles or none (but did rank candidates), it is obvious they made a mistake. At first, all of them were disenfranchised, but even after the county fixed its own mistake, 2,114 attempts to vote failed.

There is no way around the fact that RCV makes ballots longer and more complicated. This will mean longer lines at polling places and more work for polling place volunteers assisting voters. It might directly affect outcomes – for example, research suggests voters become more likely to vote "no" on ballot measures the further they are down the ballot. And RCV increases the risk that voters either make a mistake or simply give up on voting.

RCV Hurts Vulnerable Voters

Every problem for voters created by RCV is likely to fall hardest on vulnerable voters. This is ironic, since many of those pushing RCV also criticize any requirement that voters show identification in order to vote. How can obtaining and presenting identification – something almost everyone does anyway – be "Jim Crow 2.0," while learning a new voting process and using a much more complicated and longer ballot is no problem?

Consider blind voters. In a normal election, using an auditory or tactile (i.e., Braille) system, the voter indicates one choice in each race. This is a relatively simple process that can be done quickly and privately. RCV represents a major change and significant new burden. FairVote has paid the left-leaning Center for Civic Design to create model voting systems for voters who are blind or have other disabilities. The best they have come up with is a cumbersome process where the voter must rearrange the order of candidates, moving them up and down a list, which would be particularly difficult using an auditory system.

Voters with other disabilities will face similar new challenges to fully use RCV. So will voters who speak little or no English. Academic research has also confirmed that older Americans are more likely to both report and experience difficulty with RCV. Yet all these voters are told by RCV's elitist advocates that they must figure out the new ballot and election process or else risk their votes being thrown away.

Again, the irony of all this is unmistakable. The Center for Civic Design usually advocates simpler ballots to protect vulnerable voters. A presentation by its executive director,

Whitney Quesenbery, declares that "voting with a disability is a civil right." She coauthored a 2008 Brennan Center report warning that confusing ballots mean "a significant percentage of voters will be disenfranchised, and the affected voters will disproportionately be poor, minority, elderly and disabled voters."

When it comes to RCV, the question is not whether it will have a disparate impact on vulnerable voters, but how severe that impact will be. The Center for Civic Design's attempt to help FairVote develop vulnerable voter–friendly RCV systems is lipstick on a pig.

RCV is Exhausting!

Even in a normal election, voters sometimes stop voting before reaching the end of their ballot. "Ballot fatigue" is particularly common in elections with many non-partisan offices or complicated policy measures up for a vote. RCV makes this so much worse, it has led to a new term: "ballot exhaustion." This is when a voter stops voting within just one

A stable party system provides a check on demagogues.

race on the ballot. Rather than use all the possible rankings, the voter moves on (or gives up).

This is extremely common. In fact, Fair-Vote's own research suggests that 29 percent of voters in RCV elections reject RCV entirely – they "rank" just one candidate. Another pro-RCV group, Common Cause New York, published exit poll data from New York City's 2021 Democratic Party primary for mayor that shows similar results. Only 42 percent of voters there reported fully using RCV (by ranking five candidates, the maximum allowed). The effect of ballot exhaustion varied across racial groups. Black voters were 2.5 times more likely to rank only a single candidate than white voters. This increased the relative likelihood of their ballots being exhausted.

Common Cause celebrated that election as "the largest and most diverse ranked choice voting election in the United States." Nearly a million voters participated. It featured thirteen candidates, including former presidential candidate and RCV-advocate Andrew Yang. He received 115,130 first-preference votes and was not eliminated until the sixth round. Yet when the election was finished, more voters' ballots were exhausted than had voted for Yang. By the eighth tabulation, 140,202 ballots were set aside for failing to rank one of the final candidates

Some view this as disenfranchisement. Others claim these discarded ballots are the foreseeable consequence of voters' own choices. They say ballot exhaustion is like failing to show up and vote in a runoff election. But in a traditional runoff, voters know which candidates are in the final round. With RCV, it is impossible to know who will remain through the multiple rounds of tabulation. Voters are left to guess, and when they get it wrong, their "exhausted" ballots get tossed out.

Supporters of RCV admit that implementing their system will require expensive public education campaigns. The Center for Civic Design has a twenty-five-page report on how to put together RCV "education and communication materials." It notes that a "major change in elections, like implementing Ranked Choice Voting, creates a need for voter education." The report emphasizes the importance of graphics, translations, and repetition.

In New York City, this meant a $15 million voter education campaign. With all that spending, as noted above, fewer than half the voters reported fully using their RCV ballot. And while the spending included a deluge of funds for outreach to minority groups, white voters still reported using RCV more – and so likely more effectively – than other voters.

RCV supporters claim their system is easy to use. Then, when a city like New York adopts it, they rush in demanding expensive education campaigns. No doubt some of the latter is simply about directing public funding to RCV advocacy groups. But it is also an admission that even these advocates realize how difficult RCV is for many voters.

An Election Administration Nightmare

It was March of 2023 before the Oakland school board election mess was finally sorted out. A court ordered a "recertification of the results," and the rightful winner took office four months after Election Day. (The candidate who was previously sworn in had already resigned after serving on the board for about a month.) The fact is that consequential mistakes like this can happen in any large RCV election, and, in many cases, they may never be detected.

The simple fact is that RCV makes it harder to vote.

While RCV is difficult for voters, it imposes an even greater burden on election administrators. RCV's multiple rounds of counting, adjusting votes, and eliminating ballots all create additional work for election staff, and they also necessitate a new set of arbitrary election rules. Some might be determined by a legislative body, but much of this rulemaking falls to election officials.

New Rules, New Power

Are these decisions really arbitrary? Consider the specific issue in Alameda County. Hundreds of voters left the first-preference bubble blank but still ranked candidates. County election officials had to decide on a rule; staff had to program election equipment to follow that rule. One option was to treat those ballots like overvotes and toss them out. Another was to adjust the ballots before the first round, moving up a voter's rankings so that they start with a first-preference vote and do not contain any gaps.

That pre-tabulation adjustment is what

Alameda County's election rules required. But there was a third solution: ignore those ballots in the first round. That is what county election equipment actually did. And nobody at the county, nor in the competing campaigns, noticed.

Running an RCV election requires other similar decisions. Will low-performing candidates be eliminated one by one, or in batches? Will an overvote in one preference position cancel just that preference vote, or all preference votes in the race? How many rankings are allowed? How are write-in candidates dealt with? RCV creates some of these issues and makes others more complex.

What the Oakland school board race shows is that these decisions can flip the outcome of an election. There were three candidates in that race: Mike Hutchinson, Pecolia Manigo, and Nick Resnick. Under any rules, Resnick had a significant lead in the first round. One of the other candidates was going to be eliminated. With the machines applying the wrong rules and discarding 235 ballots, Hutchinson was 41 votes behind Manigo, and was thus eliminated. But when those 235 ballots were adjusted and counted according to the county's rules, Hutchinson led Manigo by 37 votes.

This completely flipped the race. Hutchinson went from being eliminated in the first round to winning. This happened because many more of the ballots that lacked a first-preference vote had Hutchinson as their highest-ranked candidate rather than Manigo. But then Manigo's voters, in their next-highest preference, supported Hutchinson over Resnick by about two-to-one.

RCV: Rise of the Machines

The Alameda County mistake shows how RCV makes elections over-reliant on technology, reducing transparency and accountability. There were 30,983 ballots in the first round of the school board election, with 26,432 recorded votes (using the recertified numbers). For the second round, 1,846 ballots were eliminated, and 6,344 votes were moved from Manigo to either Hutchinson or

Resnick. This was a relatively simple race, with three candidates and two rounds of counting. Yet doing it efficiently meant relying on computers – not just to count ballots, but to adjust and eliminate them as well.

The problem is reliance. All modern elections make use of computerized equipment.

RCV creates new possibilities for voter errors.

Yet what computers do in normal elections is pretty simple: scan votes and add them up. This simplicity means: (1) mistakes are easy to recognize; (2) humans provide a meaningful backup; and (3) ordinary voters can understand it all. These are not side issues – they are essential to maintaining trust in a democratic process.

In addition to normal vote counting, RCV requires reallocating certain votes, eliminating other votes, and then doing it all over again. The number of rounds is limited only by the number of candidates. At a large scale, doing all this by hand would require a massive effort. Oversight would be near impossible. And so pro-RCV technocrats step in with the answer: let computers do it.

The simplest computer functions, like adding numbers, are transparent – ordinary people can verify the math. Increase the complexity just a little, and transparency evaporates. Ordinary people – voters but also election observers and poll workers – cannot easily verify the results of a computer after multiple rounds of RCV adjustments. This can only lead to more voter dissatisfaction and distrust.

Recounts Anyone?

In the closest elections, or when something has gone wrong, the traditional way to confirm (or change) the result is by recounting the votes – often by hand. This is laborious even in normal elections. The Ranked Choice Voting Resource Center, a project of Fair-

Vote, admits that hand counting RCV ballots "is more complicated and time consuming than the counting for a simple plurality election." Nevertheless, it claims it can be "easily done by hand," offering only two examples from within the United States – the tiny cities of Telluride, Colorado, and Takoma Park, Maryland.

In fact, conducting a hand recount would present a massive logistical problem in any large RCV election. Hiring and training the staff required and establishing the process for a hand recount could extend beyond the deadline to certify an election.

There is also a little-noticed conflict between the RCV process and state recount laws. These often trigger or allow a recount when the final margin in an election is very close. Yet with RCV, it is not just the final margin that matters. The Oakland school board race shows how a very close result in an earlier round can lead to a much larger margin in the final result. In states that allow RCV, legislatures need to update recount laws so that any round of tabulation can trigger a recount. If RCV advocates find this onerous, that is an admission of the weakness of their proposed voting system.

The End of Transparency and Accountability in Elections?

Elitism has always been a hallmark of the push for RCV and similar voting systems. A 1914 issue of *Proportional Representation Review*, making the case for Hare's RCV system, argued that it is only complicated for election officials. Why? Because voters do not need to understand it. "The only persons who have to understand the Hare system of counting the votes are those who count them at the central electoral office."

In Alameda County, unfortunately even the people at the central office failed to understand their new system. After private researchers tipped them off to their mistake, county staff spent Christmas weekend on the phone with Dominion Voting Systems, the company that had supplied their software.

They re-ran all of the November election calculations. At some point, county officials must have breathed a sigh of relief when they learned that only one school board race had come out the wrong way.

Mistakes are toxic to democracy because they raise reasonable suspicions that election results may not accurately reflect voter decisions. RCV creates new possibilities for mistakes while making it harder to detect them. This lack of transparency threatens public trust in the process.

RCV is Even Worse by Mail

A confounding factor in Alameda County's woes is that California runs its elections by mail. This means no poll worker is there to help a voter understand the RCV process or to provide a replacement ballot. Voting by mail using RCV also means that all those extra ballot pages must be mailed – twice, at greater expense – and kept track of by the voter in between mailings.

In states that count ballots arriving days or

RCV means longer lines at polling places and more work for polling place volunteers.

weeks after election day, RCV guarantees slower results. Since small changes in early rounds of tabulation can have cascading effects that change the results in later rounds, the RCV process cannot begin until all ballots are received and processed.

ANSWERING RCV's CLAIMED BENEFITS

Unite America lists four benefits of RCV: it guarantees a majority winner, increases competition, saves money, and encourages civility. In the past, some RCV supporters have also claimed it increases voter turnout. Fair-Vote says RCV leads to more women and racial minorities winning elections. Some of these claims are based on observational case studies rather than real research and analysis. Others are simply wishful thinking. None of the claims made about RCV stand up to scrutiny.

"Majority Winners"

Unite America claims that RCV "guarantees ... that the candidate that wins the election is the one the majority of the people actually wanted." This is false.

A research paper examining RCV elections between 2004 and 2022 found that in most of the races studied, the winner had less than majority support from among the participating voters. These included a county treasurer with 37.5 percent voter support, a city council member with 36.1 percent, and even a member of the San Francisco Board of Supervisors with just 24.3 percent. The only reason RCV advocates can claim these candidates received a majority is because their system discards so many "exhausted" ballots.

Using this kind of logic, any election system can guarantee a majority winner. Just throw every ballot that does not contain a vote for one of the top two candidates and, viola! It's an RCV-style, make-believe majority.

The primary for New York City Mayor, mentioned earlier, provides another example. Eric Adams is recorded as winning with 50.4 percent of the vote. But add back in the 140,202 exhausted ballots, and he received just 42.9 percent. And either way, RCV made no difference – Adams held a significant lead in the first round and every subsequent round. In other words, the benefit of RCV in the election was a talking point about a majority winner that turns out to be false.

"Increased Competition"

According to Unite America, RCV "increases competition" by making it more likely that third-party and independent candidates receive recorded votes. This argument begs the question, because what RCV advocates dislike is not so much a lack of competition as the kind of competition that exists in American politics today. Much of that competition is within two major political party coalitions. Shifting some of it outside of those coalitions does not mean the level of competition has changed at all.

There is also no reason to suppose that preference votes for losing candidates have an effect on political competitiveness, or anything else. To its credit, FairVote's website acknowledges a 2021 study of nine cities with RCV that found "no apparent impact on ideological composition of the city councils." It would be surprising if RCV could both increase competition in elections and pro-

---

How can presenting identification be "Jim Crow 2.0," while using a much more complicated and longer ballot is no problem?

---

duce greater agreement among voters (more majority winners). As it turns out, RCV does neither.

"Saving Money"

One of the more fanciful claims of RCV advocates is that it can save money. This is a half-truth. When RCV is part of a larger change that reduces the total number of elections, costs are likely to go down. This is common sense – each election has fixed costs. But changing the election calendar and replacing normal elections with RCV are two different reforms. Often, RCV is implemented without reducing election days. In that case, costs can only increase.

Not all election equipment and software can handle RCV ballots or tabulation. This means that implementing RCV can come with steep upfront technology costs. There are also training expenses for election staff and volunteers, in addition to the public education campaigns discussed above. Some of this will be a continuing cost, as RCV elections are simply more complicated and thus will require greater training and oversight. Longer RCV ballots mean more expenses for paper, printing, shipping, and mailing, and greater wear on tabulation machines. Finally, any RCV recounts may add significant overtime costs.

"Encouraging Civility"

Politics can get nasty. It certainly was during the presidential campaign of 1800, when Thomas Jefferson's hatchet man wrote that John Adams was a "hideous hermaphroditical character." A generation later, Andrew Jackson was depicted in at least one cartoon as a demon and a newspaper alleged that his mother "was a common prostitute." If only they had RCV back then – Unite America claims it makes politics nicer "because candidates appeal to their opponent's supporters for second place votes."

This is wishful thinking. Consider the examples above. Jefferson did not sign his name to the scurrilous attack on Adams. And

Jackson's opponents (including Adams's son, John Quincy Adams) left it to their own pressmen to slander Old Hickory. Candidates have always preferred to leave negative campaign-

---

FairVote's own research suggests that 29 percent of voters in RCV elections "rank" just one candidate.

---

ing to surrogates, and RCV provides at best one more judge in that same direction.

It is worth pointing out that polls by pro-RCV groups are of little value on topics like this. The groups lobby cities to adopt RCV, promising it will make campaigns more positive. As part of voter education campaigns, they get cities to tell voters that RCV makes campaigns more positive. Then, after telling voters what to think, they survey voters and ask what they think. Whatever it is, this is not sound social science.

Turnout Games

RCV advocates also play games with data to claim their plan increases voter turnout. Turnout in a general election is almost always higher – usually substantially so – than in either primary or runoff elections. Groups like FairVote use this fact to concoct apples-to-oranges comparisons between turnout in these different kinds of elections. When RCV adoption is part of a larger plan that elimi nates a primary or runoff and reduces the total number of elections, turnout naturally goes up. All this was confirmed in an aca-demic paper entitled "Voter Participation with Ranked Choice Voting in the United States," which compared elections in cities with RCV to those with normal elections.

The truth is that changes in turnout from one election to another are usually driven by voter interest in the candidates. Turnout differences across jurisdictions seem to have more to do with culture than particular election processes. The paper mentioned above provides a list of "reforms touted as turnout boosters ... that have done little to increase voter participation," including voting by mail, early voting, and registering voters when they get a driver's license. It implies that RCV is another reform that is unlikely to deliver on promises to boost voter participation.

The truth is worse than that. RCV tries to have it both ways, claiming credit for all the voters who show up, but then throwing out some of their ballots as "exhausted." All turnout data from RCV elections should have a note indicating the number of voters who showed up but were not included in the final round votes.

How to Stop Ranked-Choice Voting

States are the fundamental level of government in the United States (as the name implies). Except where power is delegated in the Constitution to the federal government, it remains with the states. This is true for most election policy and administration, particularly for state and local elections. State legislatures have the power to limit, regulate, or prohibit the use of RCV in state and local elections.

This is important because RCV advocates target local governments first. In these smaller elections, the flaws of RCV are less noticeable. They are not shy about their goal, however, which is to implement RCV in all elections.

In 2007, the city of Sarasota, Florida, tried to implement RCV. State officials argued it violated the law and refused to certify new RCV election equipment for the city. That stopped it in Florida, until another city moved to implement RCV in 2022. The state legislature passed a bill, signed by Gov. Ron DeSantis, to end the uncertainty and prohibit the system in any Florida elections. Just a month earlier, Tennessee passed a ban on

RCV. Other states are now following their lead. In 2023, Idaho, Montana, and South Dakota passed bans on RCV, while similar legislation passed at least one chamber in Arizona, Missouri, South Dakota, and Texas.

Some states also have constitutional provisions that interfere with RCV. Ironically, Maine is one of those. While using RCV for many elections, it cannot use it in general elections for state offices, because the Maine Constitution happens to specify that those elections must be by plurality. Enforcing or adding state constitutional protections is one way to block RCV. Enacting statutory bans, as in Florida and Tennessee, is another.

Even where RCV is used, voters can demand its repeal. This has happened many times. RCV was in place for just one election cycle in Aspen, Colorado, before voters rejected it there in 2010. The year before, voters repealed RCV in one of Washington state's largest counties after just three years. As this book goes to print, a campaign in

Alaska is likely to put repeal on the ballot there in 2024.

Americans want elections where it is easy to vote and hard to cheat. RCV makes it harder to vote, and harder to trust and verify the process. While America has done away

---

Consequential mistakes can happen in any large RCV election, and, in many cases, they may never be detected.

---

with poll taxes and literacy tests for voting, RCV represents a step backwards. It makes voting especially harder for those who already face challenges to vote. It also imposes new burdens on election administrators.

RCV advocates forget that elections are not just for experts. The simplicity of an election system is part of what makes it democratic. It also allows the process to be transparent and trustworthy. The push for RCV threatens further to erode the public trust that is the bedrock on which democracy stands – or falls.

First American edition published in 2023 by Encounter Books, an activity of Encounter for Culture and Education, Inc., a nonprofit, tax-exempt corporation.
Encounter Books website address: www.encounterbooks.com

Manufactured in the United States and printed on acid-free paper. The paper used in this publication meets the minimum requirements of ANSI / NISO z39.48–1992 (R 1997) (*Permanence of Paper*).

FIRST AMERICAN EDITION

Library of Congress Cataloging-in-Publication Data is available for this title under the ISBN: 978-1-64177-369-0 and the LCCN: 2023941393